The Countries

Venezuela

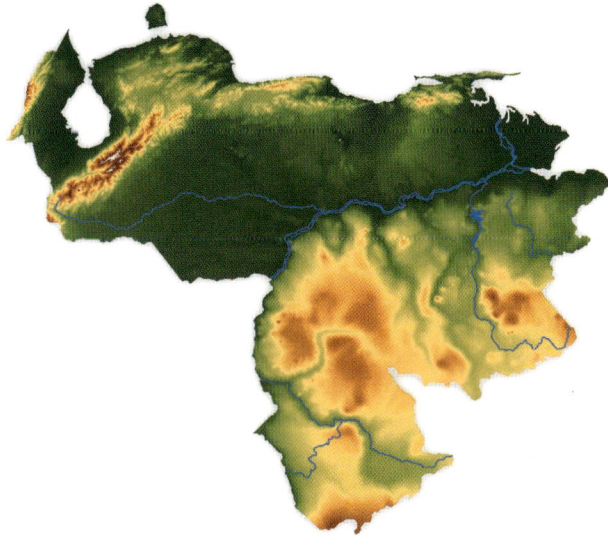

Kate A. Conley

ABDO Publishing Company

visit us at
www.abdopub.com

Published by ABDO Publishing Company, 4940 Viking Drive, Edina, Minnesota 55435.
Copyright © 2004 by Abdo Consulting Group, Inc. International copyrights reserved in
all countries. No part of this book may be reproduced in any form without written
permission from the publisher.

Printed in the United States.

Photo Credits: AP/Wide World p. 6; Corbis pp. 5, 8, 9, 11, 12, 13, 16, 18, 19, 20, 21, 22,
     23, 24, 27, 29, 31, 32, 33, 35, 36, 37

Editors: Stephanie Hedlund, Kristianne E. Vieregger
Art Direction & Maps: Neil Klinepier

Library of Congress Cataloging-in-Publication Data

Conley, Kate A., 1977-
    Venezuela / Kate A. Conley.
        p. cm. -- (The countries)
    Includes index.
    Summary: An introduction to the history, geography, plants and animals, people,
economy, cities, transportation, government, sports and leisure activities, and
holidays and festivals of Venezuela.
    ISBN 1-59197-298-1
    1. Venezuela--Juvenile literature. [1. Venezuela.] I. Title. II. Series.

F2308.5.C66 2003
987--dc21
                                                             2003040333

Contents

¡Hola!

Hello from Venezuela! Venezuela is a tropical nation located in South America. Its beautiful land stretches from the Caribbean Sea to the Andes Mountains.

Venezuela's land has a vast supply of **petroleum**. This has become an important part of the nation's **economy**. It made Venezuela one of South America's richest nations.

Throughout its history, Venezuela has been home to many kinds of people. Native peoples, African slaves, and Spanish colonists have all settled there. They have created a **culture** unlike any other in the world!

Today, Venezuelans face many challenges. The nation's government is unstable, and many people are poor. Despite these problems, Venezuelans are working together to make their country a wonderful place to live.

Hola *from Venezuela!*

Fast Facts

OFFICIAL NAME: Bolivarian Republic of Venezuela
(República Bolivariana de Venezuela)
CAPITAL: Caracas

LAND
- Area: 352,144 square miles (912,049 sq km)
- Mountain Range: Andes Mountains
- Highest Point: Pico Bolívar 16,427 feet (5,007 m)
- Major River: Orinoco River

PEOPLE
- Population: 24,287,670 (July 2002 est.)
- Major Cities: Caracas, Maracaibo
- Languages: Spanish (official), Indian dialects, English
- Religions: Roman Catholicism, Protestantism

GOVERNMENT
- Form: Federal republic
- Head of State: President
- Head of Government: President
- Legislature: National Assembly
- Nationhood: July 5, 1811

ECONOMY
- Agricultural Products: Corn, sorghum, sugarcane, rice, bananas, vegetables, coffee; beef, pork, milk, eggs; fish
- Mining Products: Petroleum, iron ore, bauxite, gold, diamonds
- Manufactured Products: Food, textiles, steel, aluminum, motor vehicles
- Money: Bolívar (1 bolívar = 100 centimos)

Venezuela's flag

Venezuela's money

Timeline

1498	Christopher Columbus arrives in present-day Venezuela; Spain soon makes Venezuela a colony
1811	Venezuelans declare their independence from Spain
1819	Venezuela joins with Colombia and Ecuador to form Gran Colombia
1821	Simón Bolívar's forces finally defeat Spain at the Battle of Carabobo
1830	Venezuela leaves Gran Colombia and becomes an independent nation
1900s	Venezuelans discover oil in their land
1920s	Venezuela is the world's largest oil exporter
1947	Venezuela holds its first free election
1992	Colonel Hugo Chávez unsuccessfully tries to overthrow the government
1998	Chávez elected president
2002	Venezuelans try to overthrow Chávez, but he returns to office

Venezuela's Past

People have lived in Venezuela for thousands of years. Some of Venezuela's native people were **nomads** who hunted and gathered food. Others lived in small farming villages.

Many natives lived in Venezuela when Christopher Columbus arrived there in 1498. Columbus was an explorer who worked for Spain. He was the first European to arrive in Venezuela.

Spain controlled Venezuela and made it a colony. At first, the Spaniards used Venezuela as a place to fish for pearls and capture natives to use as slaves. Later, the Spaniards established plantations and imported African slaves to do the plantation work.

Christopher Columbus

Venezuelan leaders declare themselves independent from Spain.

During Spain's rule, Spaniards held top positions in Venezuela's government and church. **Creoles** controlled the land. Natives, slaves, and people of mixed backgrounds had little power in the colony.

Venezuelans declared their independence from Spain on July 5, 1811. A Creole named Simón Bolívar led the independence movement. His forces finally defeated Spain at the Battle of Carabobo in 1821. Bolívar's forces also helped liberate Colombia, Ecuador, Peru, and Bolivia.

Venezuela formed a **republic** with Colombia and Ecuador in 1819. It was called Gran Colombia. In 1830, Venezuela left Gran Colombia and formed an independent nation.

For more than 100 years, military **dictators** ruled Venezuela. These dictators were called caudillos (kow-DEE-yohs). The caudillos established reforms, such as permitting religious freedom. Yet they also created **civil wars** and political disorder.

In the early 1900s, Venezuelans discovered oil in their land. By the 1920s, the country had become the world's largest oil exporter. However, the money from the oil made only a few people rich. Many other Venezuelans lived in poverty.

During the oil boom, caudillos remained in power. Then in 1945, Rómulo Betancourt took over the government. He led a political party that wanted to create a **democracy** in Venezuela. In 1947, Venezuela held its first free election. Author Rómulo Gallegos won.

Shortly after Gallegos took office, the military overtook the government. A military **dictator**, Marcos Pérez Jiménez, took office. He ruled until 1958, when the military restored **democracy** in Venezuela.

Rómulo Gallegos was not only a leader of Venezuela's government, but he was also a world-famous novelist.

With **democracy** restored, Venezuelans elected Betancourt president. He governed Venezuela from 1959 to 1964. During that time, he tried to improve the nation's health care, farming methods, and **literacy** rates.

Throughout the 1960s and 1970s, Venezuela's democratic government worked well. Its **economy** grew as the world demanded more oil.

Hugo Chávez

Then in the late 1970s, oil prices dropped. Venezuela's economy suffered, and people began to protest.

In 1992, Colonel Hugo Chávez led a **coup d'état** (koo-day-TAH). It failed, and Chávez went to jail. He was later released, and in 1998 Venezuelans elected him president. The next year, he rewrote the nation's **constitution**, giving many powers to the president.

Chávez's changes angered many Venezuelans. This led to protests and violence. In April 2002, he ordered the army to silence protesters. Twelve protesters died in the process. In response, military leaders removed Chávez from office. Two days later, however, he was back in power.

In December 2002, strikes became so large that the oil industry suffered. In fact, Venezuela actually had to import oil from other countries! By February 2003, however, many companies had resumed business. Today, Chávez continues to face protests. He and all the citizens of Venezuela must work together to restore peace to their country.

Many protesters believe that Chávez has too much power. They fear this will further hurt the economy and people.

Land of Beauty

Venezuela is in South America. The country's neighbors are Colombia, Brazil, and Guyana. The Caribbean Sea and Atlantic Ocean border northern Venezuela. Several islands in these waters are part of the nation as well.

Hills and valleys cover southern Venezuela. This land is rich in iron ore, gold, and diamonds. Southern Venezuela also contains Angel Falls. It is the world's highest waterfall.

Plains called the Llanos (YAH-nohs) cover central Venezuela. Soil in the Llanos is poor. So, farmers use the flat, grassy land to raise cattle.

The Llanos give way to the Andes Mountains in the north. Pico Bolívar rises out of the Andes. This snowy peak is Venezuela's highest point.

Northern Venezuela also contains Lake Maracaibo (mah-rah-KAI-boh). The shallow lake is actually a large sea inlet. Its shores are a major source of **petroleum**.

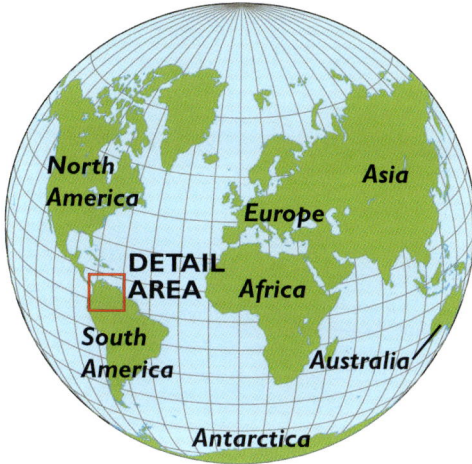

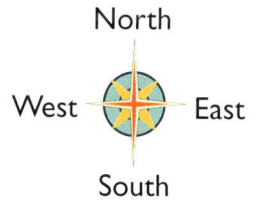

A tour boat on the Orinoco River

Venezuela's only desert lies near a northern town called Coro. Strong winds have formed miles of sand dunes there. A national park protects the dunes.

Venezuela's major river is the Orinoco. It begins near the Venezuela-Brazil border and flows across much of the nation. The river empties into the Atlantic Ocean.

Venezuela has a warm climate with two seasons. The dry season lasts from December to April. The rainy season lasts from May to November.

Rain

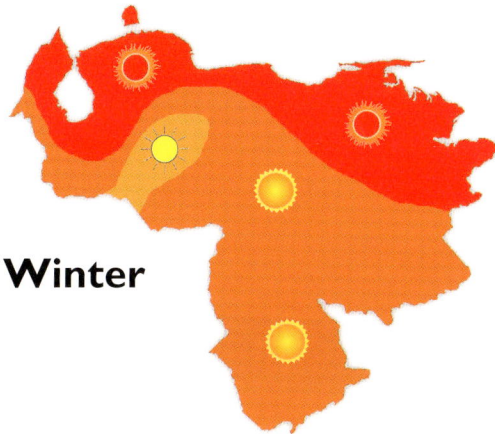

Winter

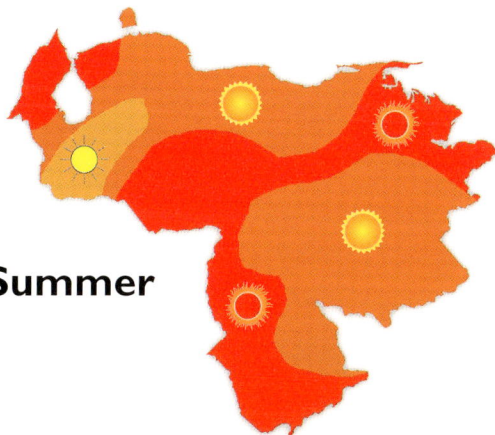

Summer

Rainfall

AVERAGE YEARLY RAINFALL

Inches		Centimeters
Under 10		*Under 25*
10 - 20		*25 - 51*
20 - 40		*51 - 102*
Over 40		*Over 102*

North

West   East

South

Temperature

AVERAGE TEMPERATURE

Fahrenheit		Celsius
Over 80°		**Over 27°**
65° - 80°		**18° - 27°**
50° - 65°		**10° - 18°**
32° - 50°		**0° - 10°**

Plants & Animals

Venezuela's land supports many different plants. Grasses cover about half of the nation's land. Tropical rain forests grow in Venezuela's lowlands. Evergreen forests line the banks of the Orinoco River.

In the mountains, the plants vary by elevation. Forests with ferns and orchids grow between 3,000 and 6,000 feet (914 and 1,829 m). Higher up, grasses replace the forests. These grasses give way to small shrubs at the highest elevations.

Trees along the Orinoco River

Many unique birds live in Venezuela, such as this scarlet macaw.

Venezuela also has many interesting trees. The tonka tree produces scented beans. They are used to make perfume. The araguaney (ah-rah-GWAH-neh) is Venezuela's national tree. Yellow blooms cover the araguaney at the end of the dry season.

Many animals live in Venezuela. Wildcats such as jaguars, ocelots, and pumas live there. Alligators and crocodiles live in the rivers. Venezuela is also home to birds such as parrots, toucans, pelicans, and flamingos.

Venezuelans

About 23 million people live in Venezuela. Most Venezuelans are mestizos. Mestizos are people who have European, Indian, and African ancestors.

A young violinist practices with the National Children's Orchestra in Caracas.

Several Indian tribes also live in Venezuela. The tribes are scattered throughout the country. The Guajiro (gwah-HEE-roh) is the largest tribe. Its members live near the city of Maracaibo.

Nearly all Venezuelans speak Spanish. It is the country's official language. English is a popular second language in Venezuela's largest cities. Many of Venezuela's Indian tribes continue to speak their native languages.

Venezuelans have a unique culture because so many different people have come to live together in their country.

Venezuela's **constitution** grants its people religious freedom. Some Indian tribes continue to practice traditional religions. But, many Venezuelans are Roman Catholic.

Children in Venezuela begin school around age seven. They must attend school for six years. Some choose to continue their education for another four years. Then, some students take a course for a year to prepare for a university.

Venezuelans wear clothing similar to styles in the United States and Canada. Men often wear dress shirts and khaki pants. Women often wear dresses or blouses and skirts. Students in public and private schools wear uniforms.

Children do not always have to wear their uniforms. They often dress up for special occasions.

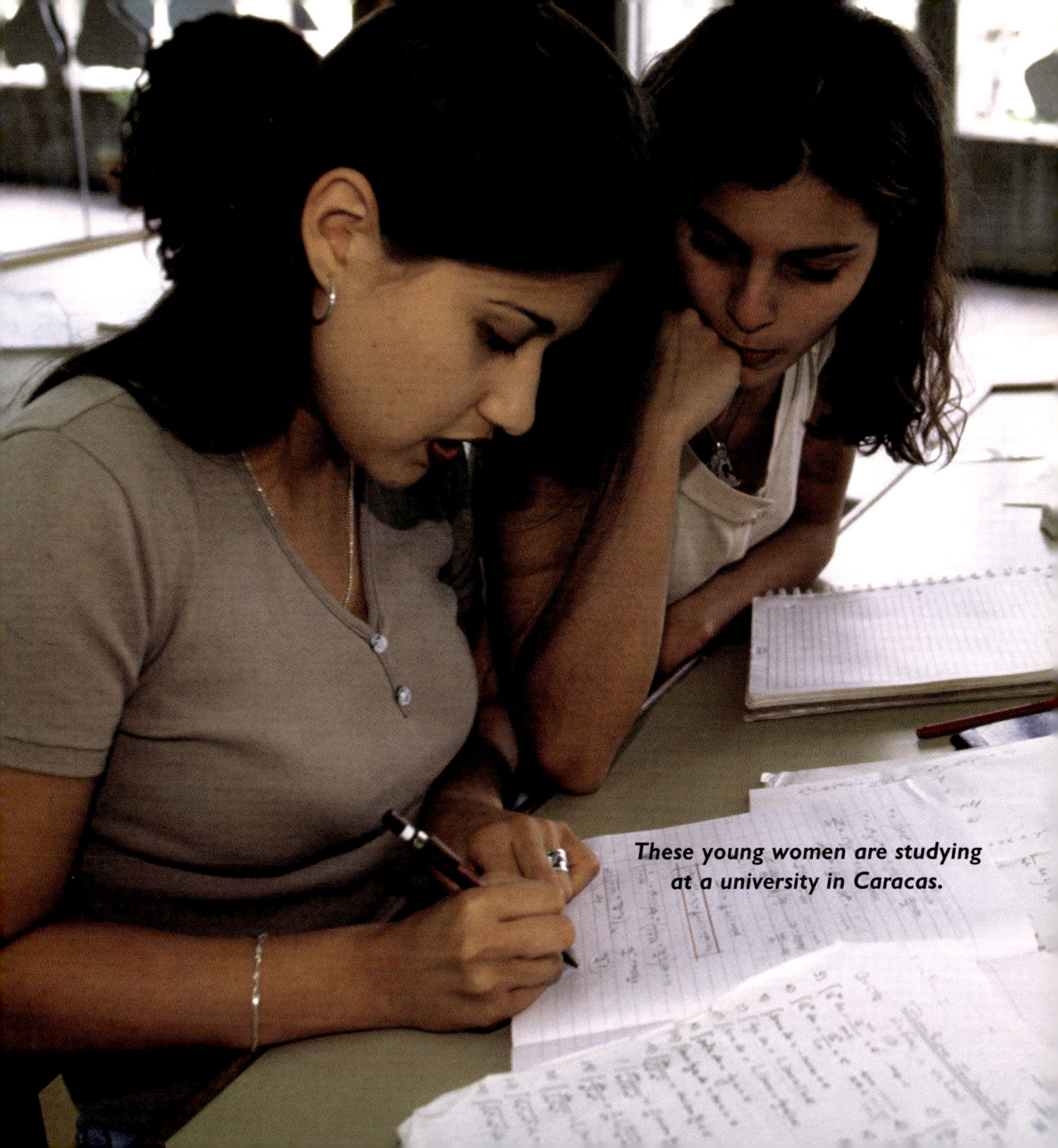

These young women are studying at a university in Caracas.

Bakeries and other small shops in the cities allow for variety in Venezuela's dishes.

Venezuelans cook many delicious dishes. *Arepas* (ah-RAY-pahs) are a common meal. They are round, flat breads made from corn flour. Venezuelans often slice *arepas* and fill them with cheese and meat.

Another popular meal is *pabellón criollo* (pah-beh-YOHN KRYOH-yoh). It is Venezuela's national dish. This meal includes shredded beef, white rice, cheese, black beans, and fried plantains.

Torta de Jojota

These delicious corn cakes are enjoyed by many Venezuelans.

- I can of cream-style corn
- 3 eggs
- 1/2 cup butter
- 2 tablespoons flour

- I cup sugar
- 1/2 cup milk
- vanilla extract (to taste)
- sugar (to sprinkle over the cake)

Mix all the ingredients in a blender. Pour the mixture in a cake pan and place it in the oven at 350°F (177°C) for one hour. Sprinkle sugar over the cake. It can be served hot or cold.

AN IMPORTANT NOTE TO THE CHEF: Always have an adult help with the preparation and cooking of food. Never use kitchen utensils or appliances without adult permission and supervision.

LANGUAGE

English	Spanish
Hello	Hola (OH-lah)
Please	Por Favor (POHR fah-VOHR)
Girl	Chica (CHEE-kah)
Boy	Chico (CHEE-koh)
Friend	Amigo/Amiga (ah-MEE-goh/ah-MEE-gah)

Earning a Living

Venezuela's **economy** is based on producing and exporting **petroleum** products. But, petroleum is not Venezuela's only valuable natural resource. The nation is also rich in minerals, such as iron ore and bauxite. Venezuela also has deposits of gold and diamonds.

Water is another important natural resource in Venezuela. Water-generated energy provides more than half of the nation's electricity. Guri Dam is Venezuela's most important source of waterpower. It is the second-largest dam in the world.

Farming is also part of Venezuela's economy. Farmers grow bananas, sugarcane, corn, coffee, and cacao (kuh-KOW). Venezuela's government has also developed the nation's industry. Factory workers produce cars, chemicals, clothing, and food.

Opposite page: Many people work hard to keep an oil-drilling rig functioning.

Caracas & Maracaibo

Caracas is Venezuela's capital and largest city. It is located in a long, narrow valley near the Caribbean Sea. About 5 million people call Caracas home.

Caracas is a mix of new and old. The city has many modern skyscrapers, office buildings, and apartments. Yet, it also has many historic places, such as the home where Simón Bolívar was born.

Maracaibo is Venezuela's second-largest city. Its location near Lake Maracaibo makes it a major port. Maracaibo is also an important source of **petroleum** and minerals.

Near Maracaibo is Sinamaica Lagoon. There, many people live right above the lagoon in homes built on stilts. Indian tribes have been living this way for hundreds of years.

In 1499, explorers Alonso de Ojeda and Amerigo Vespucci sailed past these homes. They reminded the explorers of the canals in Venice, Italy. So, they called the area Venezuela, which means "little Venice."

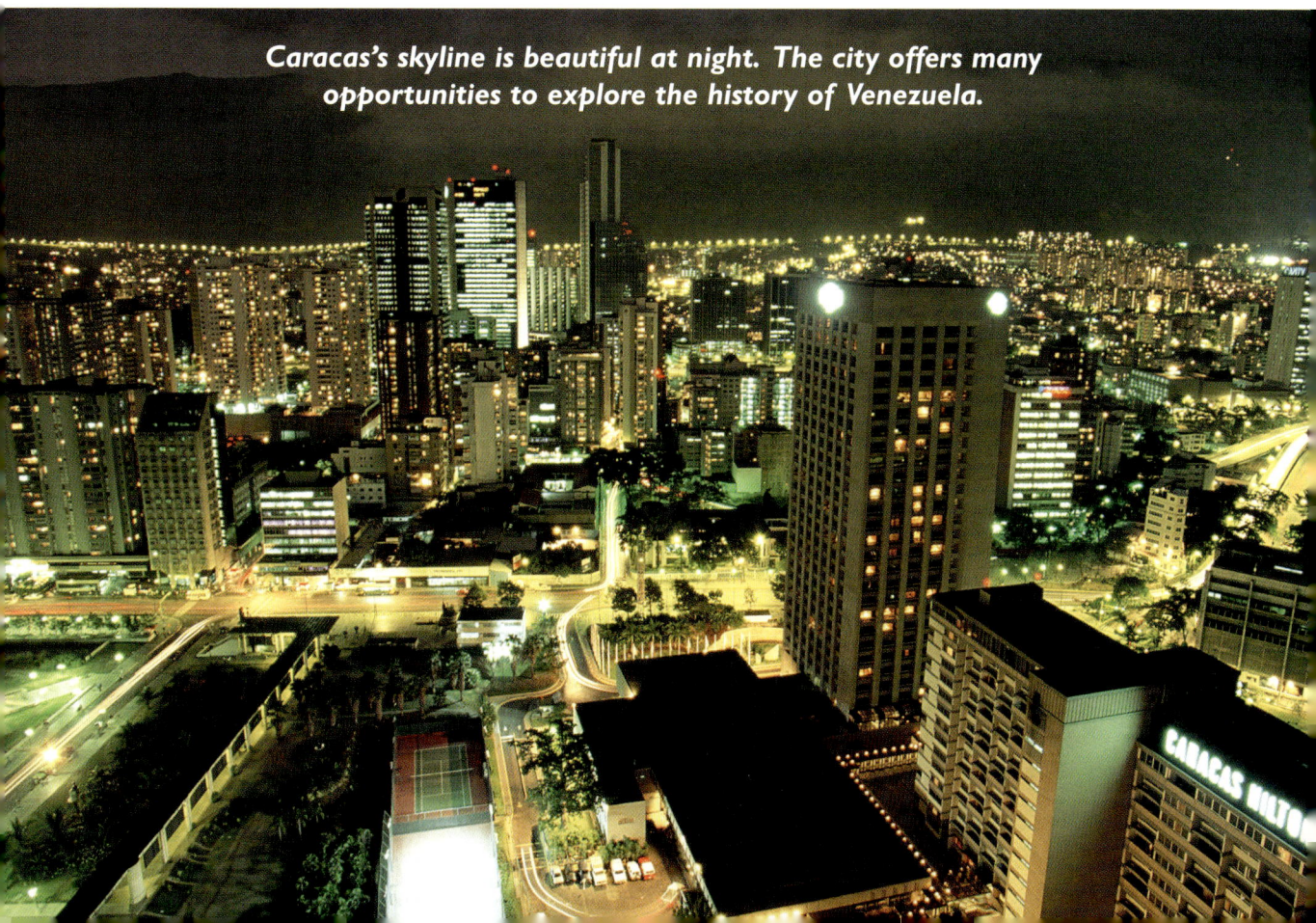

Caracas's skyline is beautiful at night. The city offers many opportunities to explore the history of Venezuela.

Getting Around

Venezuelans have many ways to travel from place to place. People usually take a bus or an airplane when they go on long trips. For shorter trips, Venezuelans often drive, walk, bike, or ride local buses.

Venezuela's local buses are often minibuses or vans. Depending on the region, they may be called *busetas*, *carritos*, or *micros*. Local buses cost little to ride, but they are often very crowded.

In Caracas, many people ride on the city's subway system, which is called the metro. The metro carries passengers across the city. It is a clean, safe, and fast way to travel in Venezuela's capital.

Ships also play an important role in Venezuela's transportation system. Ships transport many of Venezuela's goods. These ships travel to ports along the country's coast and Lake Maracaibo.

Subways in Venezuela offer people a safe and easy way to travel through the city.

Venezuela's Government

Venezuela is a federal **republic**. It has 23 states, one federal district, and one federal dependency. Each state elects its own governor.

Venezuelans elect a president to a six-year term. In 1999, Venezuela received a new **constitution**. It grants the president many powers. The president serves as the head of government and head of state. The president can appoint people to the cabinet.

Venezuelans elect 165 people to serve five-year terms on the National Assembly. Assembly members make Venezuela's laws. They also elect the members of the Supreme Court.

A tour group inside the Capitolio Nacional

Venezuela's government is represented in many international organizations. One of the most well-known groups is the Organization of the **Petroleum** Exporting Countries (OPEC). OPEC is a powerful group of oil-producing nations. They work together to keep prices stable and make sure there is a steady supply for consumers.

The Capitolio Nacional, located in Caracas, is both a historic museum and the seat of the government.

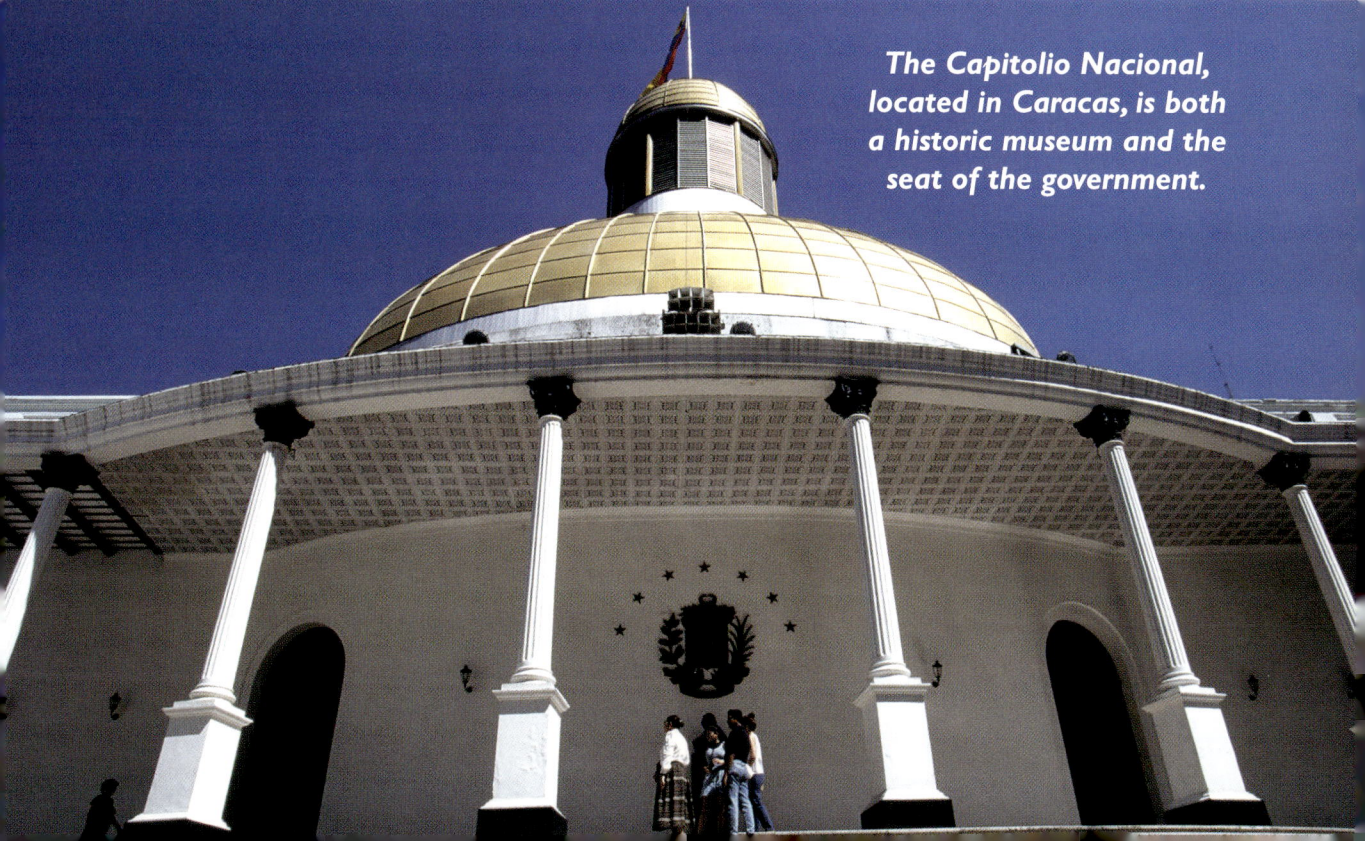

Time to Celebrate!

Throughout the year, Venezuelans celebrate many different festivals and holidays. National holidays include Independence Day on July 5, Simón Bolívar's birthday on July 24, and Discovery of America on October 12.

In addition, Venezuelans celebrate many religious events. Nearly every town has its own **patron saint**. On the day devoted to the town's saint, people celebrate with feasts, church services, bullfights, and beauty **pageants**.

One of Venezuela's major festivals is Carnaval. It takes place just before **Lent**. During Carnaval, people dress up in costumes and wear masks. Many people attend parades, listen to music, and go dancing.

Christians celebrate the mother of Jesus.

At Christmas, Venezuelans often go to the beach or stroll through their neighborhoods. Many also eat a traditional Christmas meal called *hallacas*. *Hallacas* are made from cornmeal dough filled with meat, vegetables, and seasonings. They are wrapped in banana leaves and steamed.

Relaxing

Venezuelans relax in several different ways. Many Venezuelans enjoy watching baseball. It is the country's most popular sport. Venezuela has a professional baseball league with eight teams. Children also like to play games at local baseball diamonds.

Many Venezuelans also love music. The country's most popular folk music is called *joropo* (hoh-ROH-poh). *Joropo* singers accompany a harp, a small guitar, and rattles. *Joropo* began in the Llanos. Today, one *joropo* song called "Alma Llanera" has become an unofficial national **anthem**.

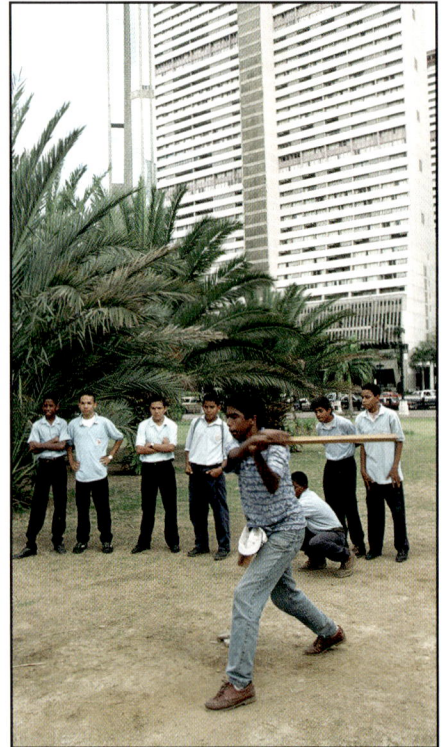

Local baseball games are often a big part of growing up in Venezuela.

Beauty **pageants** are another popular activity in Venezuela. The country has produced several Miss Universe and Miss World winners. Many have gone on to have successful careers. For example, one former winner named Irene Sáez ran for president against Hugo Chávez in 1998.

Irene Sáez was crowned Miss Universe in 1981. After her reign, she worked on her political career.

Watching television is another **pastime** in Venezuela. Soap operas, called *telenovelas* (tay-lay-no-VAY-las), are popular programs. Many people make time in their work and social schedules to watch their favorite *telenovela*.

Glossary

anthem - a song of gladness or patriotism.

civil war - a war between groups in the same country.

constitution - the laws that govern a country.

coup d'état - a sudden, violent overthrow of a government by a small group.

Creole - a person of Spanish or French descent who was born in Latin America or the West Indies.

culture - the customs, arts, and tools of a nation or people at a certain time.

democracy - a governmental system in which the people vote on how to run their country.

dictator - a ruler with complete control who usually governs in a cruel or unfair way.

economy - the way a nation uses its money, goods, and natural resources.

Lent - the 40 weekdays before Easter.

literate - able to read and write.

nomad - a member of a tribe that moves from place to place.

pageant - a presentation of contestants in which they are judged on talent and beauty.

pastime - something that makes time pass happily.

patron saint - a saint believed to be the special protector of a church, city, state, or country.

petroleum - a thick, yellowish black oil. It is used to make gasoline.

republic - a form of government in which authority rests with voting citizens and is carried out by elected officials, such as those in a parliament.

Web Sites

To learn more about Venezuela, visit ABDO Publishing Company on the World Wide Web at **www.abdopub.com**. Web sites about Venezuela are featured on our Book Links page. These links are routinely monitored and updated to provide the most current information available.

Index